DALLAS COWBOYS · SUPER BOWL CHAMPIONS

VI, JANUARY 16, 1972
24-3 VERSUS MIAMI DOLPHINS

XII, JANUARY 15, 1978
27-10 VERSUS DENVER BRONCOS

XXVII, JANUARY 31, 1993
52-17 VERSUS BUFFALO BILLS

XXVIII, JANUARY 30, 1994
30-13 VERSUS BUFFALO BILLS

XXX, JANUARY 28, 1996
27-17 VERSUS PITTSBURGH STEELERS

SUPER BOWL CHAMPIONS

DALLAS COWBOYS

AARON FRISCH

CREATIVE EDUCATION

COVER: WIDE RECEIVER MICHAEL IRVIN

PAGE 2: QUARTERBACK DON MEREDITH AND COACH TOM LANDRY

RIGHT: DEFENSIVE END ED JONES KNOCKING DOWN A QUARTERBACK

Published by Creative Education
P.O. Box 227, Mankato, Minnesota 56002
Creative Education is an imprint of The Creative Company
www.thecreativecompany.us

Book and cover design by Blue Design (www.bluedes.com)
Art direction by Rita Marshall
Printed by Corporate Graphics in the United States of America

Photographs by Corbis (Dana Hoff), Dreamstime (Rosco), Getty Images (Diamond Images, James Drake/Sports Illustrated, Nate Fine/NFL, Focus On Sport, Scott Halleran, Hunter Martin, Ronald Martinez, Al Messerschmidt/NFL, George Rose)

Library of Congress Cataloging-in-Publication Data

Frisch, Aaron.
Dallas Cowboys / by Aaron Frisch.
p. cm. — (Super Bowl champions)
Includes index.
Summary: An elementary look at the Dallas Cowboys professional football team, including its formation in 1960, most memorable players, Super Bowl championships, and stars of today.
ISBN 978-1-60818-016-5
1. Dallas Cowboys (Football team)—History—Juvenile literature. I. Title. II. Series.

GV956.D3.F75 2011
796.332'64097642812—dc22   2009053501

CPSIA: 040110 PO1141

First Edition
9 8 7 6 5 4 3 2 1

CONTENTS

SUPER BOWL CHAMPIONS

Dallas is a city in Texas. Dallas sits on a hot prairie and is sometimes called "Big D." The Dallas area has a **stadium** called Cowboys Stadium that is the home of a football team called the Cowboys.

COWBOYS FACTS

First season:
1960

Conference/division:
National Football Conference, East Division

Super Bowl championships:
VI, January 16, 1972 / 24-3 versus Miami Dolphins
XII, January 15, 1978 / 27-10 versus Denver Broncos
XXVII, January 31, 1993 / 52-17 versus Buffalo Bills
XXVIII, January 30, 1994 / 30-13 versus Buffalo Bills
XXX, January 28, 1996 / 27-17 versus Pittsburgh Steelers

Training camp location:
San Antonio, Texas

NFL Web site for kids:
http://nflrush.com

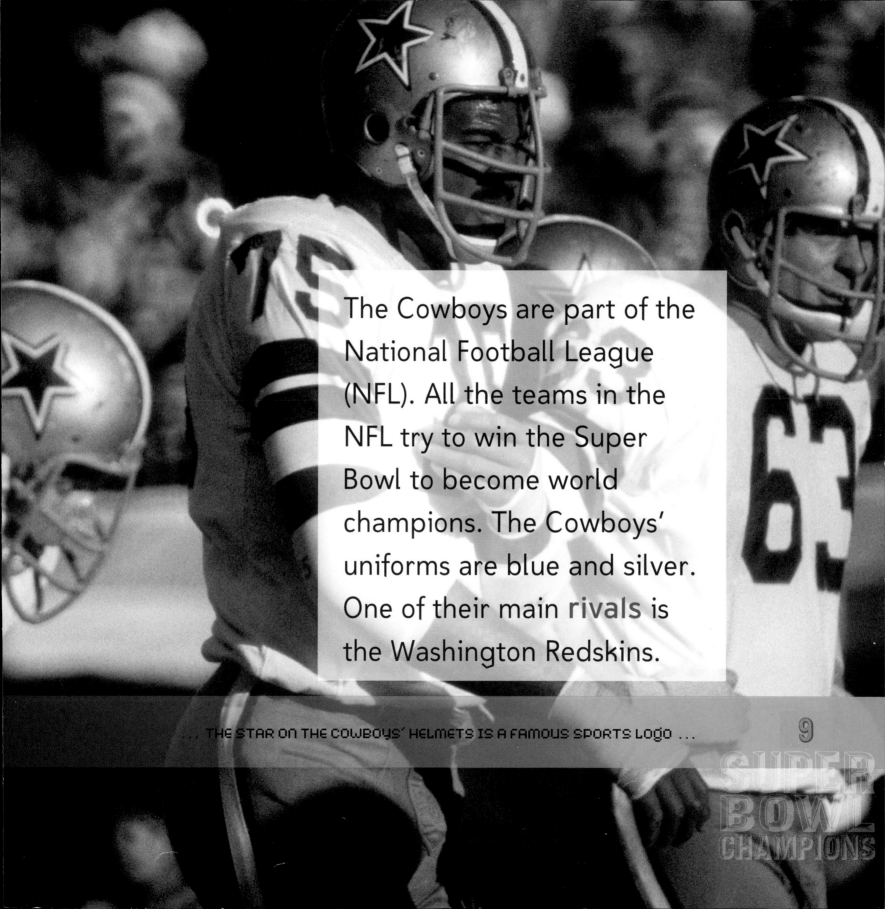

The Cowboys are part of the National Football League (NFL). All the teams in the NFL try to win the Super Bowl to become world champions. The Cowboys' uniforms are blue and silver. One of their main **rivals** is the Washington Redskins.

The Cowboys played their first season in 1960. Their first coach was Tom Landry. He coached the Cowboys for 29 seasons. In 1964, Dallas added a smart quarterback named Roger Staubach.

... ROGER STAUBACH WAS GOOD AT ESCAPING FROM DEFENSIVE PLAYERS ...

SUPER BOWL CHAMPIONS

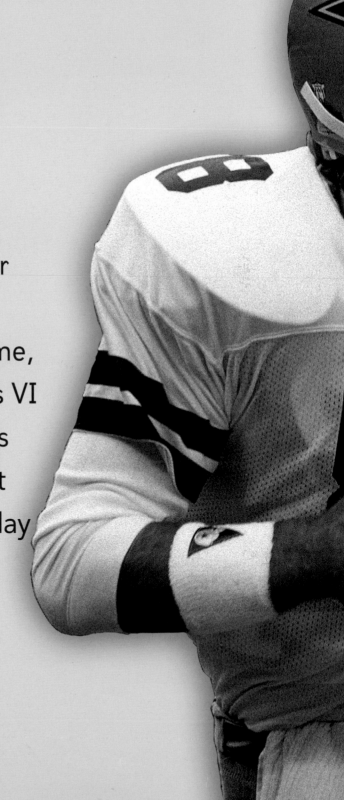

The Cowboys got to Super Bowl V (5) after the 1970 season. They lost that game, but they won Super Bowls VI (6) and XII (12). The Dallas defense was so tough that fans called it the "Doomsday Defense."

SUPER BOWL CHAMPIONS

The Cowboys were not as good in the 1980s. But in the 1990s, new stars like receiver Michael Irvin and quarterback Troy Aikman came to Dallas. They helped the Cowboys win Super Bowls XXVII (27), XXVIII (28), and XXX (30).

SUPER BOWL CHAMPIONS

The Cowboys made the **playoffs** many seasons after that. Fans cheered for players like tight end Jason Witten, who played in the **Pro Bowl** almost every year. But Dallas could not reach the Super Bowl again.

... JASON WITTEN MADE 94 CATCHES FOR THE COWBOYS IN 2009 ...

15

Two of the Cowboys' first stars were Bob Lilly and Bob Hayes. Lilly was a strong defensive tackle. Hayes was a wide receiver who ran so fast that fans called him "Bullet Bob."

... BOB HAYES (LEFT) AND BOB LILLY (RIGHT) ...

SUPER BOWL CHAMPIONS

17

WHY ARE THEY CALLED THE COWBOYS?

Texas has always had a lot of ranches with horses and cattle. Cowboys are tough men who do such work as taming wild horses and herding cattle.

SUPER BOWL CHAMPIONS

In 1977, the Cowboys added quick running back Tony Dorsett. One game, he ran 99 yards for a touchdown! Emmitt Smith was an even better running back. He set an NFL **record** for the most rushing yards ever.

... DeMARCUS WARE WAS A TALL LINEBACKER WITH GREAT SPEED ...

Dallas added linebacker DeMarcus Ware in 2005. In 2008, he made 20 **sacks**. That was the most in the NFL. Dallas fans hoped that he would help lead the Cowboys to their sixth Super Bowl championship!

SUPER BOWL CHAMPIONS

SUPER BOWL CHAMPIONS

GLOSSARY

playoffs — games that the best teams play after a season to see who the champion will be

Pro Bowl — a special game after the season where only the NFL's best players get to play

record — something that is the best or most ever

rivals — teams that play extra hard against each other

sacks — plays where a player tackles a quarterback who is trying to throw a pass

stadium — a large building that has a sports field and many seats for fans

23

INDEX